Iguanodon

by Grace Hansen

DINOSAURS

Abdo

Kids

abdopublishing.com

Published by Abdo Kids, a division of ABDO, P.O. Box 398166, Minneapolis, Minnesota 55439.

Copyright © 2018 by Abdo Consulting Group, Inc. International copyrights reserved in all countries. No part of this book may be reproduced in any form without written permission from the publisher.

Printed in the United States of America, North Mankato, Minnesota.

052017

092017

THIS BOOK CONTAINS RECYCLED MATERIALS

Photo Credits: Alamy, iStock, Science Source, Shutterstock, Thinkstock, ©user:Ballista p.21 / CC-BY-SA-3.0

Production Contributors: Teddy Borth, Jennie Forsberg, Grace Hansen

Design Contributors: Dorothy Toth, Laura Mitchell

Publisher's Cataloging in Publication Data

Names: Hansen, Grace, author.

Title: Iguanodon / by Grace Hansen.

Description: Minneapolis, Minnesota : Abdo Kids, 2018 | Series: Dinosaurs |
    Includes bibliographical references and index.

Identifiers: LCCN 2016962380 | ISBN 9781532100383 (lib. bdg.) |
    ISBN 9781532101076 (ebook) | ISBN 9781532101625 (Read-to-me ebook)

Subjects: LCSH: Iguanodon--Juvenile literature. | Dinosaurs--North America--
    Juvenile literature.

Classification: DDC 567.914--dc23

LC record available at http://lccn.loc.gov/2016962380

Table of Contents

Iguanodon. 4

Body 8

Climate & Food 18

Fossils 20

More Facts 22

Glossary 23

Index 24

Abdo Kids Code. 24

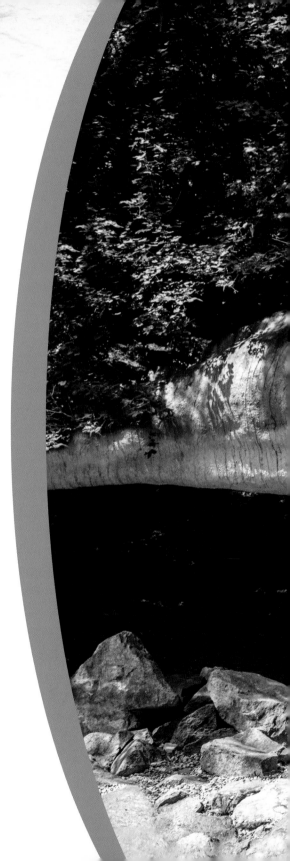

Iguanodon

Iguanodon lived during the early Cretaceous period. That was around 125 million years ago.

4

Iguanodon was an **ornithopod**.

It ate plants.

Body

Iguanodon could grow up to 16 feet (4.9 m) tall. It weighed around 10,000 pounds (4,536 kg)!

9

Iguanodon had thick hind legs.

It had short, skinny arms.

Each arm ended in four fingers and a claw. The claws were probably used for eating and fighting.

13

Iguanodon walked on all four limbs. It may have run on its back legs. It used its long tail for **balance**.

15

Iguanodon had a small head.
It plucked leaves with its beak.
The back of its mouth was full
of teeth. Iguanodon was very
good at chewing its food.

Climate & Food

The **climate** was very warm and wet when Iguanodon was alive. There were lots of plants for Iguanodon to eat.

19

Fossils

Iguanodon **fossils** have been found around the world. The first were found in 1822 in England. More fossils have been found in Europe, Africa, and North America.

20

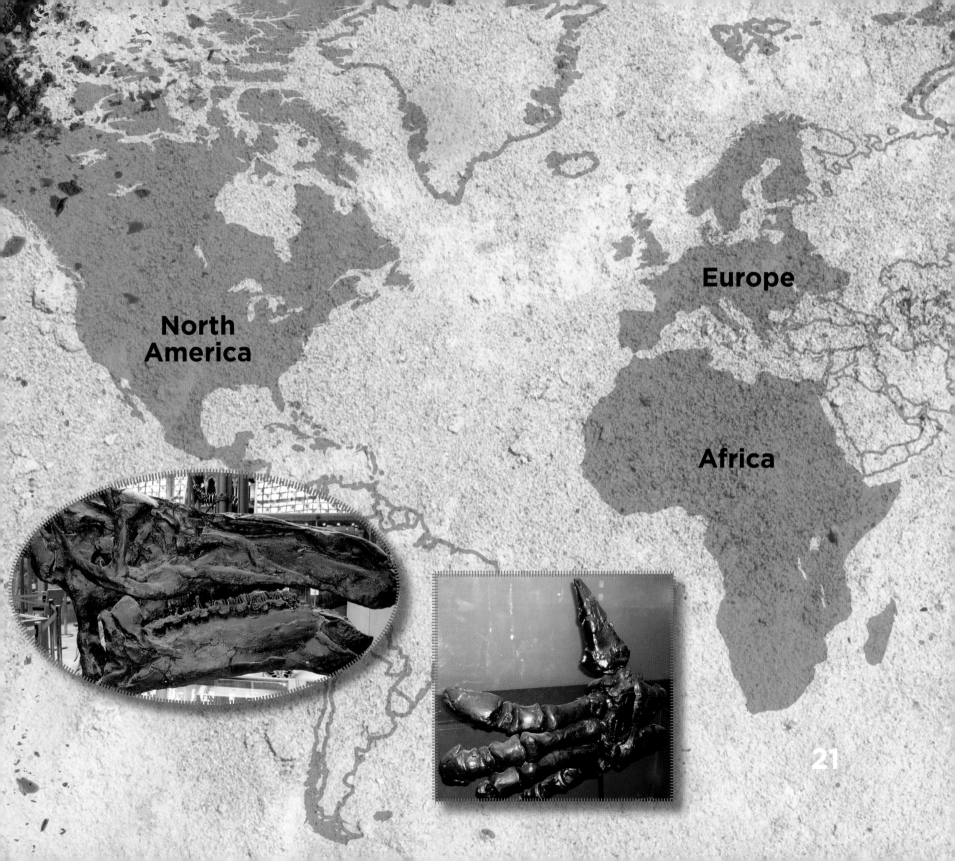

North America

Europe

Africa

21

More Facts

- Iguanodon means "iguana-like teeth." The first fossils found had teeth that look like an iguana's, except much larger.

- Preserved footprints found in southern England showed that these dinosaurs traveled in groups and walked upright.

- Iguanodon's unique thumb spikes were thought to be horns that grew from the dinosaur's head. Fossil scientists learned where the spikes went when they found more complete remains in the 1870s.

Glossary

balance – an even distribution of weight to remain upright.

beak – the hard, pointed part of some dinosaurs' mouths.

climate – the weather in an area for a long period of time.

Cretaceous period – rocks from the Cretaceous period often show early insects and the first flowering plants. The end of the Cretaceous period, about 65 million years ago, brought the mass extinction of dinosaurs.

fossil – the remains, impression, or trace of something that lived long ago, as a skeleton, footprint, etc.

ornithopod – a plant-eating dinosaur that often walked or ran on its hind legs.

Index

Africa 20

arms 10, 12, 14

beak 16

claws 12

Cretaceous period 4, 18

England, United Kingdom 20

Europe 20

food 6, 12, 16, 18

fossils 20

habitat 18

head 16

legs 10, 14

mouth 16

North America 20

ornithopod 6

size 8

tail 14

teeth 16

abdokids.com

Use this code to log on to abdokids.com and access crafts, games, videos and more!

Abdo Kids Code:
DIK0383